WITCH

For Cristyn,
who asks me: are there witches?

DAMIAN WALFORD DAVIES
WITCH

SEREN

Seren is the book imprint of
Poetry Wales Press Ltd.
57 Nolton Street, Bridgend, Wales, CF31 3AE
01656 663018
www.seren-books.com
Facebook: facebook.com/SerenBooks
Twitter: @SerenBooks

The right of Damian Walford Davies to be identified as
the author of this work has been asserted in accordance
with the Copyright, Designs and Patents Act, 1988.

© Damian Walford Davies 2012

ISBN: 978-1-85411-579-9

A CIP record for this title is available from the British Library.

The publisher acknowledges the financial assistance of the Welsh Books Council.

Cover image by Clive Hicks-Jenkins www.hicks-jenkins.com

Printed in Bembo by CPI Group (UK) Limited, Croydon

Thomas Love	Priest
Nicolas Strelley	Gentleman
Absalom Strelley	Son of the Above
John Jendring	
Jane Humfrey	
Isabel Gage	
Miles Daniel	Villagers
Thomas Gowd	
Giles Selwyn	
Ellen Haye	
Clemence Addy	Labourer
Alyce Addy	Daughter of the above
Francis Hurst	Discoverer of witches
Valentine Lind	Judge of Assize

Part One
February to April 1643

Thomas Love

We're in Domesday: meadow,
fallow, plot and gravel pit,

flintwork church a little to the east;
Great House and cherry grove;

damson orchards blemishing
the light; the river slick

with fish; those millsails beating
on the pent-up pond. Beyond

lies corn-earth draining
to the sea. Even on rafty days,

keen eyes can see five spires –
God's needles tacking up the dark.

My garden borders on the deadfold
where they murder down the lambs.

Drifts of soldiery: fairy rings
of last night's fires in the wood,

crosshatch piles of tiny bones,
comet-tails of baggage trains.

Outlandish meetings in the lanes.
Today I saw two strangers fowling

on the common, low sun striking
off their snares. I raised my hand.

They gathered up a brace of snipe,
barred bodies in a limp embrace,

and stood there, watching. Lent,
at least, is bringing in more light.

I note this intimately at the fire
with Zekiel, my pious little marmoset.

The light struck Alyce differently
this evening, entering through

rich glass to dye and dapple her.
I saw tendrils of the Jesse Tree

about her hair, the Saviour's
lacerated yellow sallowing her cheek.

I laid the wafer on her tongue,
her neck blebbed with the bad thief's

blood. Her mother watched me
from the dark. I made a homily

on the candle's flame, sickly now
and wanton in the flood

of so much light. They listened;
but whether my correlations held...

Wet from burying old Varley
in a shroud he saw his daughter

bleed to spin and stitch,
I carried in the gravesoil

on my boots. In the hall
the clay is curing into dust,

marking where I wavered,
caught between my wife's lips

and my daughter holding up
her doll – a moment of un-

balance, tiny caracole and slip
between two objects worthy

of a kiss. It dries dark
and hard beneath the nails.

I'm reading *Heaven's Hue and Cry*.
Whoever cut the woodblock

had a canny hand: see how the hanged
man's kicking creases up his clothes,

the out-of-kilter of his lover's neck,
bell-shape of her generous skirt,

the feet like clappers shaking out
their sin. Doubly inked below them

are the bodies of the men they
spoiled. The author says

the City's spent; I like his whack
of Revelation, but his style is flushed.

Zekiel claps the thundering,
though sometimes hides his eyes.

At the House tonight, talk
turned from martyrs to the pale

son's bought commission.
The father led him clinking

down the corridor, absurd in
spurs, an orange sash the only

nod to living, eyes waning
in his helmet's cage. I saw myself

distended in his breast-plate,
clinched hands like monstrous

clubs. His linen collar queered
all that steel. They took me

to the doorway, one in tattered
slippers, the son in roaring boots.

They came early – out of fenland –
the horses' scabby haunches

twitching in the sun, apple-blossom
carpeting a way to church.

Starting with the brasses,
they scratched out all the prayers

they could not say, made me clout
St Michael off the bench-end,

file the poor *popish apples*
of the mermaid's breasts, held

my hand that hauled the wych-
elm Man of Sorrows to the ground.

Called themselves God's carpenters.
Handed me a bill for *making good*.

Part Two
May to July 1643

Nicholas Strelley

This house had priest-holes,
black setts for badgered Jesuits.

My father blocked them up.
They still ring when I knock.

I found Love in my chancel
snivelling in his spangled

smock. The morning staged it
perfectly: he saw me at the doorway

doused in light. My slippers milled
the hunks of plaster near the font.

I said: *Now – see God's house
in nakedness!* He was nursing

bits of painted wood. I said again:
Get up! this new light rinses you.

Absalom, grey son: I watch you
through the leadlights

loiter near the herb-beds, close
your eyes, breathe lavender,

valerian. Each diamond pane
distends you into health.

Summer will green this garden.
Buckle on; war may make

you. I see you jiggered
by the whizzing of a bee, retreat

and cock your head to read
the dazzle of the little fountain

in its bowl. Absalom, framed
misty through my coat of arms.

Wanting my eaves scruffed clear
of swallows' nests, I sent him up

a year ago today. A bird flared
out across his face – he pitched –

and fell. That night his rumpled
wife came calling with a randy

tongue, flung great clots of earth
at Absalom, held him by the cuffs.

A flitting likeness of my late wife
sickened me. The birds have built

from clay again, the paths are
rank with shit. I dream of

fledglings flailing in the shambles
of a skull. Let them. Let them be.

I tell my son one war's beyond
our hot horizon. He squints

across the mowers' auburn
eddies to the haze. The other's

here, I say. He smiles. His eyes
are on the Addy woman's daughter,

bent in no-man's-land beside
the gate. Alone, her mother's

in the middle of the field, a blue
rag wadded round her head,

grass in spills of silver at her feet.
The others cut around her

gingerly. She straightens, brazen –
sunburnt in her aftermath.

Bitter herbs embitter me. What
harmony this house possessed

is soured by each next spiteful
remedy for Absalom. Most things

he vomits up: spheres of pepper,
pestled leaves of arsesmart,

elder bark. His water's riddled
daily at the window, muslin

straining in the light. His body
leaves no hollow on the coverlet.

She touched him. I shocked
the priest with that, made him

pray against malevolence,
wormwood drying on the beams.

I simply offer these as facts.
Her squalling at my door,

her hands on Absalom. His
sickening. His empty armour

on my wall. Her cast, her
cadging. Her randomness

at church. My household's
sourness; this summer's

savage dreams. Love's ham-
tongued service at the grave.

And other signs. Let me
English it for you: my boy

died parched. Accuse?
I simply offer them as facts.

Call my early rides a beating
of the bounds. She came

towards me on the causeway,
flaunting spears of loosestrife

from the marsh. My horse
shucked, stammered – pitched

me into rippling weed.
From the brink she offered

flowers. Sodden, I saw
my wife again, a woman

on a slender lip of land
drawn shrill against the sky.

Her purple petals dazzled. *Love!*
I tendered. Then I said it: *witch*.

Part Three
August to October 1643

John Jendring, Jane Humfrey, Isabel Gage, Miles Daniel,
Thomas Gowd, Giles Selwyn, Ellen Haye

I hoodwink them with killing-pips
in balls of rankling beef. A rat

will drag its belly home to die,
the bright green berry burning

in its gut. I've opened nests
to see dark bodies thrash

like fish until the tail lies stiff
and separate. Then the nub

of henbane's in the whole brood's
blood. Dark bread in ale works

best for moles. I stroke them,
hold them to the light to see

their black's not altogether black
before I nail them to the fence.

What if my lips were stained
with juice? Is there a law

they must be eaten in a pie?
Who's she to say I'd gorged

myself and looked as if I'd
coughed up blood? *You'll*

want to bathe those bramble
wounds, indeed. She held

the fattest berry to my face
and ran a finger round its globes,

each one, she said, a perfect
world. And then the gall to ask

for some. I gave her none. Why
else would scratches turn to scars?

The bonny legs slipped clear,
dancing to the mother's

thrusts. When the dimpled
breech and arms were free

it seemed the little one was
pushing too, hands braced

against the bloody thighs.
In the curl of steam and giddy

tang of spearmint, we saw
the boy's trunk blanch. It was

Addy pushed two fingers in
to hook the cord, drew out

the head, pursed her lips
and blew until he bawled.

Didn't I thank her for the gift
of what she calls her breath?

I've woken in the dark
to find her hanging over me,

lips parted, gurgling – gross
tongue tugging at its roots,

birthblood in bright stipples
on her breasts. Her speech

is thirsty, snatched: *Miles,
my love, my wicked tinker-*

boy, my bear, my weasel.
My wife stirs next to me;

in the crib the baby's
chest moves up and down.

His cocking thumb left smears
of powder on the playing cards.

He raised his piece. We'll give
you one, he said, to blow out

Charlie's golden brains; a horse
that doesn't shy at shot,

a metal skin; and girls to lick
the grazes clean. He seized

my wrist; held the candle
to my fan of cards. Ash wisps

hung between us on the air.
She bent beside him, jaws

working at his ear. He let my
hand fall, smiled. Began to cry.

She's pert, but it's the girl
I'd take the marshy road

to skirt. I watched her hup
herself into the orchard,

lie against a tree and roll
two damson stones around

her mouth to mock me
through the hurdle's cuts

of light. Scratch her; draw
the badness from that gipsy

hide. Today I caught her
canting in my crop,

making whorling sallies
through my cunny-blasted corn.

We were eeling in the fingers
of the creek, drawing knots

of muscle from the rushwork
creels, a silty tidemark just

above the knees. We watched
him loll along the boards,

lank sprays of loosestrife
in his hands. Clem dropped

her trussed skirt on the tide,
two eels flailing round

her wrists, quickening water
lapping at our legs. He saw us,

held his poor posy out. *Love!*
he said. I couldn't say to which.

Part Four
November 1643

Thomas Love, Alyce Addy, Clemence Addy

Come in. Quickly. Let me bar
the door against this blight

of leaves. Won't you sit?
Wait – I'll put Zekiel on his

chain – save you picking
wrecks of walnut cases

from your hair. Some orange
steep? – hot, clovey, honeyed –

just the thing to oust this
bitterness. See him praying

on his perch? – He'll – look –
cross himself and hold his

fingers up to bless. Forgive
me. This is difficult to say.

These days we lose the light
too early from this room.

Your plot looks west, I think?
I'm jealous! Drink. Please.

I'll start again. This heart-
shaped parish is a wheel.

I mean, there's centre and
circumference, crux and edge.

Let me put it differently: be
neighbourly, your own good

selves. Recall the church –
the clumsy lovely wood

and oafish stone they took
the hammer to last Spring.

The church? I like it better
now without those tawny

devils feeding souls
to ugly fish. I like the stir

of opened space, the way
the whitewash sears my

eyes. I've seen you watch me
through the screen, the time

it takes to lay God's body
on my tongue; your brute

itch after. My mother sees it,
too. Your monkey's chafing

at his chain. This posset's
cloying, curdled. Over-spiced.

You're unaccountable. Watched
you? Yes, I've watched you rise

to the bait, and relish it. Now
they're saying you keep half

the host, and spend yourselves
against the chancel wall.

Play on: become the thing
they take you for; be cryptic;

hone their panic at the smile
withheld, the greeting not

repaid. Just remember: sour
men grow crueller in winter.

Fidgeting? Look at me.
Your mother hasn't said a word.

I'll talk. You use expensive
speech but haven't said

the word. They used to come
with coughs and cancers,

thorny births and layings
out. I know them, every

scabbed and puckered
inch. The air was seasoned

with their spite. You have
your petty hankerings;

I nurse my hurt and hunger,
too. Forgive yourself.

I count one, two, three
lost spirits in this room.

You know how close a passing
brings us: our trades pivot

on a common joint. I give you
laundered flesh. Start by burning

fennel seed. Goose grease frees
a bloated finger of its ring.

Stiff nightshirts must be cut
away. If limbs are dog-legged,

crabbed, I crack them; then
I bathe the body as I'd scour

myself, and clothe it fresh.
Unseeing, you read over them:

How are the dead raised up?
And with what body do they come?

No. I see more than you.
They've laid off fighting

for the frost, but malice
hasn't gone to ground.

I want to say it, feel it
lash around the mouth:

witch, witch. – How does
that plain word sound,

that whip of air between
us? You'll say my dead

pitch robs it of its clout.
I could say it viciously,

expel the breath
until you heard it hurt.

Part Five
December 1643 to January 1644

Francis Hurst

One must sometimes suffer
fools. *But Mr Hurst*, one bleated,

thick with beer, *aren't there
better ways to make a living,*

*now the ground is iron, than
to ferret all the wenny girls*

*the devil jumps to keep this
climbing cold away?* I said: He lies

with them, but doesn't thrill
the body – being, you see,

a spirit who condenses viscid
air. They feel him as a clammy

weight. He doesn't *jump.* As for
cold, sir, I am God's own fire.

And sundry small expenses,
over and above. You hesitate.

Why then invite me?
Your letter found me tying up

loose ends towards the coast,
where salt air seasons sin but

gives the just man's hunt new
savour. You know of my successes

there. If there is wickedness,
I'll wrench it by the roots; if not,

I'll saddle up and call you blessed.
My methods startle you? I back

them in a recent tract: *Christ's
Hammer, or, The Witch Laid Bare.*

Searchers: revel in the name.
Your business is implied

in Exodus and Acts. I possess
a deftness in this field myself,

but today we'll make it
woman's work. Look in

flagrant as in secret spots
for little lengths of flesh

that may be wrung like
fingers of a glove. Blood,

then milky liquor, can be
fondled out. Distract her —

prick the place. You'll find it
deadened if she's given suck.

Let's talk again about lewd
dreams and scars, of blight

and pest; of Jane, Giles, Miles
and Absalom. Sit up. I won't

ask again. Let's listen for a skitter
in the corner, reedy buzzing

in this souring air. What bodies
do your shucklings take?

They must be starving now.
And do you bed them down

on wool? I've seen them climb
inside a girl. I couldn't say what

time it is. I'll be relieved at six.
Let me tell you how you feel.

Let's talk about the day
your father fell. I've been

thinking of that final
endless arc. In my mind

he scrabbles for the trellised,
sunlit wall that kicks

unhurriedly away.
How do you miss him?

Does he steal up, shattered,
in the fields? My father

will be ninety, come July.
All of which to say:

are you your mother's
girl? You have her eyes.

A gratifying night, not only
for the thinning of her mettle

and the tears. A man less
on the stretch would not have

noticed it. I must append
a rider to the section headed

'Sentinels'. It was subtly done:
a slackening of the frame,

bare parting of the knees.
She shut her eyes and smiled,

as if whatever worked there
thrilled her, utterly. A minute

and she flinched, as if it bit. That,
I've never seen. I must revise myself.

Your Love's a sot. I swear
he laid an early morning

ambush, moiling at me
through the table-tombs

like some fat puck. *Walk
with me,* he said. Three

petty strides between
the yews for every one

I took. He pressed me
like a 'torney. Cant.

Uncovenanted stuff.
Know the law? I am

its very instrument. The sun
rose behind his back.

Part Six
February to March 1644

Valentine Lind

This spring Circuit
is my Passion. Take that

how you will. I quibble
to purge myself of double-

mindedness before I'm shod
with cut-steel buckles,

doused in black and scarlet
silks. I can smell the shires

on each north-easterly;
the ram-jam jails

need drawing off. There
are troopers in my train

who'll churn to mud
my Via Dolorosa out of town.

They whipped the horse
that threw me till its croup

was wattled red. I laughed
to hear them say it was

a sign. I lug the curtains
close against the dark, gulp

claret to drown the drums
that beat me into town.

There's something fretful
in the heartwood

of this house. Last night
I dreamt I was the gilded

prison angel striking
Peter from his chains.

Piquant always; but today
this ad hoc hall brews

spite. The gallery's
a mass of gums; blood

dances to the jeers.
Jury, petty gentlemen –

we gather in a baiting pit,
matted bodies at the bar.

A lawyer's psalm
will swear you in.

Lord, save us from
deceitful lips;

hide us in pavilions
from the strife of tongues.

Now you talk of effigies
in wax, hearts pricked

with hawthorn pins; yesterday
they were clay, and burned.

You say the shitting house
she drew in dust outside

your door and squatted in
was fretted; this morning

it's knifed with pocks,
like peas. Forgive me

if I fail to understand
your litany of paps and pups.

Tell me again about the black
man and his hollow voice.

I catch her tugging
at her mother's sleeve.

I'm quizzing her about
the blackbirds, and the tiny

tinselled things, like seeds;
how they found her lying

lengthened like a sow so
Jack and Pidge and Saladin

could suck. *Jack skipped,*
the mother says, and *settled*

on a nettle! The daughter
looks to me for remedies,

wrings her apron
like my little girl.

Everywhere spoken against.
Except for Love. How

allegorical. My court's
become a masque, fodder

for ballad sheets –
Hear how mournful Love

appealed to Valentine!
When the tallymen

took their seats, I read
the upshot in their eyes.

Reaching for the cloth,
I might have quipped:

our sentence on the mother
makes a sweet jest of her name.

Sucking a pearl-white
chicken bone as if

the marrow held God's
blood, he read the latest

reckonings – *Bail; Prison;*
Place in service; Fine;

Whip; Fine; Pardon;
Before judgement,

dead; Whip; Execute;
Discharge; Dicharge;

Fine; Pardon; Fine;
Whip; Whip; Discharge –

chin glib with grease.
I hadn't asked.

Part Seven
March 1644

Thomas Love

She was threshing out
a prayer from deep inside

her chained throat's
gabble. The air was dizzy

with her dirt. *Which art,*
she kept repeating,

which art in, as if the once
lithe tongue were damned

to dwell on it. Hustling
clouds let sunlight flush

in pools; she sprang
and chased it, thwacking,

thwacking back again
along her jangling leash.

Did they expect she'd
partner them in one

last meek pavane?
She scratched and bit,

lapsed sullen. At the gate
they bound her wrists

until the knot was
knuckled like a fist

and dragged her bucking
in the dirt. I followed

in her rut and fierce
curlicues, like the carving

of the vine stock's sudden
flourish into grapes.

Shouldered like a sheaf,
bare hockshins shocking

white, she felt the press
of bodies pitching up

against the pikes. Each
rung made her trussed

bulk skip. He botched
the roping-up, the halter

like a bridle round her
mouth. She turned to him

with squally eyes. Her feet
on his, he held her like

a husband by the waist,
and let her go.

Small queer motions
of her arms and then

the bowels gave. She kinked
for breath, strays

scrapping in the gaps
between her kicks,

bitter catcries catching
in her throat. The lash

spun, tightened, slowed,
unspooled. A quince-eyed

boy held out a stone;
I wrung it in my palm.

Warm and darker
when she came to rest.

Zekiel took the lemon
from the bowl, and bit.

The fruit discharged
in bitter, blinding mist.

He bared his gums,
the shocking dog-teeth

devilish. I saw the grey
tongue flutter in its

gross, ribbed groove,
the body judder;

then the fit was past.
He cocked his head

and ambled over,
fawned delightfully; bit.

Christwhite early in the hedges
where the girl's just

gone to ground. I saw her
near her mother's patch,

the once plumb spine
inclining, heft slung

brown and ragged
on her back. I called; I even

followed to the girdle
of the wood but lost her,

somehow, in the subfusc
of the scrub. There's no lure

in Christ's hard, dry,
round body from my hand.

We're in Domesday: meadow,
fallow, plot and gravel pit,

flintwork church a little to the east;
Great House and cherry grove;

damson orchards blemishing
the light; the river slick

with fish; those millsails beating
on the pent-up pond. Beyond

lies corn-earth draining
to the sea. Even on rafty days,

keen eyes can see five spires –
God's needles tacking up the dark.

My garden borders on the deadfold
where they murder down the lambs.

Acknowledgements

Some of these poems first appeared in *Poetry Wales* and *New Welsh Review*.

There is a growing literature – both critical and creative – on the making of the Early Modern witch, and I am indebted to a number of books for a deeper understanding of the tensions, stresses and fears that drove small societies to demonise those who were in various ways marginally placed. Works by the following have been particularly inspiring and enlightening: Philip C. Almond; Jonathan Barry; J. S. Cockburn; Malcolm Gaskill; Marion Gibson; Clive Holmes; Louise Jackson; Alan Macfarlane; J. A. Sharpe; Keith Thomas; Deborah Willis; Pip and Joy Wright. There is no substitute for reading the witchcraft pamphlets themselves, however; a good selection is Marion Gibson's *Early Modern Witches: Witchcraft Cases in Contemporary Writing* (2000). Warm thanks to John Barnie, Matthew Francis, Richard Marggraf Turley and Kevin Mills for their expert eyes, and ears.

About the Author

Damian Walford Davies was born in Aberystwyth in 1971. His first solo collection, *Suit of Lights* (Seren, 2009), was a Wales Literature Exchange 'Bookshelf' Choice. He has been published widely in magazines, and is a regular reader at poetry festivals in the UK. A translator and broadcaster as well as a poet and prose writer, he is Head of the Department of English & Creative Writing at Aberystwyth University, where he has taught since 1997.